P.U. YOU STINK

By R. FRIEND

Illustrated by Bill Ross

SUNFLOWER SEEDS PRESS

TWO BOOKS!
TWO BOOKS!!
TWO BOOKS IN ONE!!!
(Top) PROSE ages 6-11
(Bottom) POETRY ages 2-5
There's more than one way
to read this book!

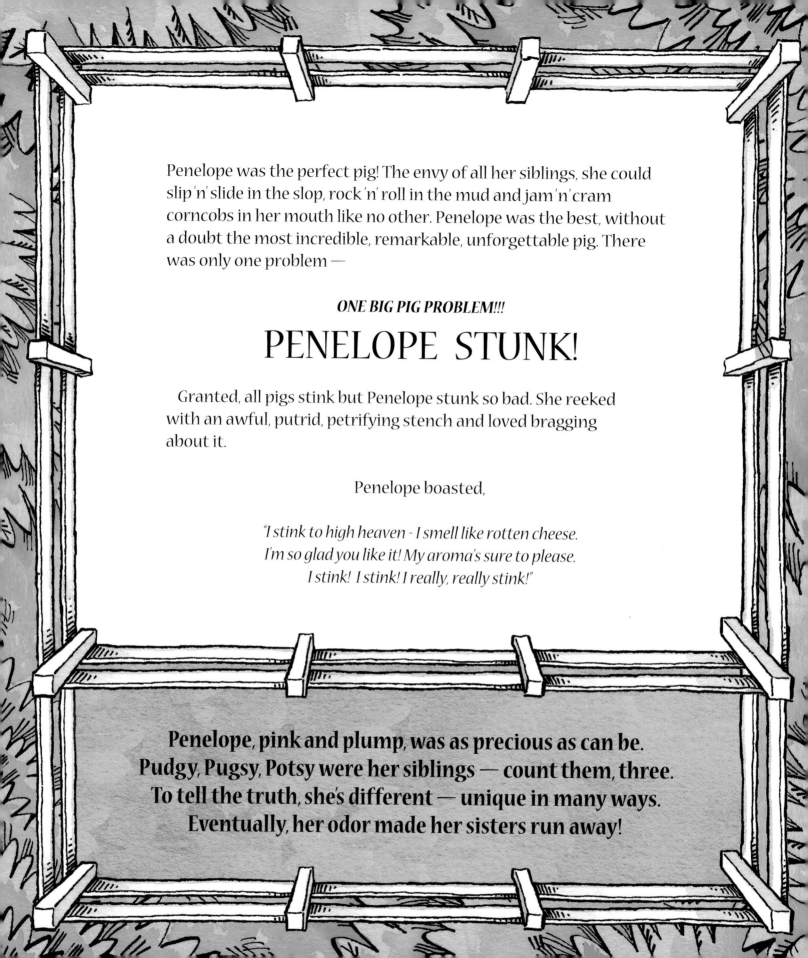

Penelope was the perfect pig! The envy of all her siblings, she could slip 'n' slide in the slop, rock 'n' roll in the mud and jam 'n' cram corncobs in her mouth like no other. Penelope was the best, without a doubt the most incredible, remarkable, unforgettable pig. There was only one problem —

ONE BIG PIG PROBLEM!!!

PENELOPE STUNK!

Granted, all pigs stink but Penelope stunk so bad. She reeked with an awful, putrid, petrifying stench and loved bragging about it.

Penelope boasted,

"I stink to high heaven - I smell like rotten cheese.
I'm so glad you like it! My aroma's sure to please.
I stink! I stink! I really, really stink!"

Penelope, pink and plump, was as precious as can be.
Pudgy, Pugsy, Potsy were her siblings — count them, three.
To tell the truth, she's different — unique in many ways.
Eventually, her odor made her sisters run away!

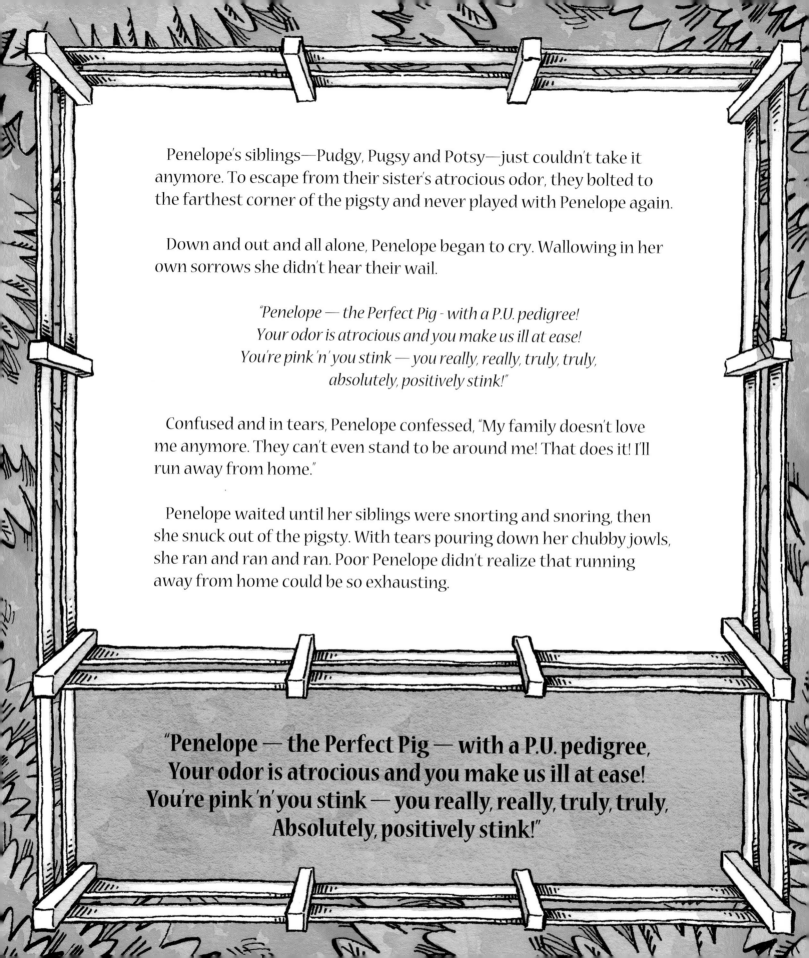

Penelope's siblings—Pudgy, Pugsy and Potsy—just couldn't take it anymore. To escape from their sister's atrocious odor, they bolted to the farthest corner of the pigsty and never played with Penelope again.

Down and out and all alone, Penelope began to cry. Wallowing in her own sorrows she didn't hear their wail.

"Penelope — the Perfect Pig - with a P.U. pedigree!
Your odor is atrocious and you make us ill at ease!
You're pink 'n' you stink — you really, really, truly, truly,
absolutely, positively stink!"

Confused and in tears, Penelope confessed, "My family doesn't love me anymore. They can't even stand to be around me! That does it! I'll run away from home."

Penelope waited until her siblings were snorting and snoring, then she snuck out of the pigsty. With tears pouring down her chubby jowls, she ran and ran and ran. Poor Penelope didn't realize that running away from home could be so exhausting.

"Penelope — the Perfect Pig — with a P.U. pedigree,
Your odor is atrocious and you make us ill at ease!
You're pink 'n' you stink — you really, really, truly, truly,
Absolutely, positively stink!"

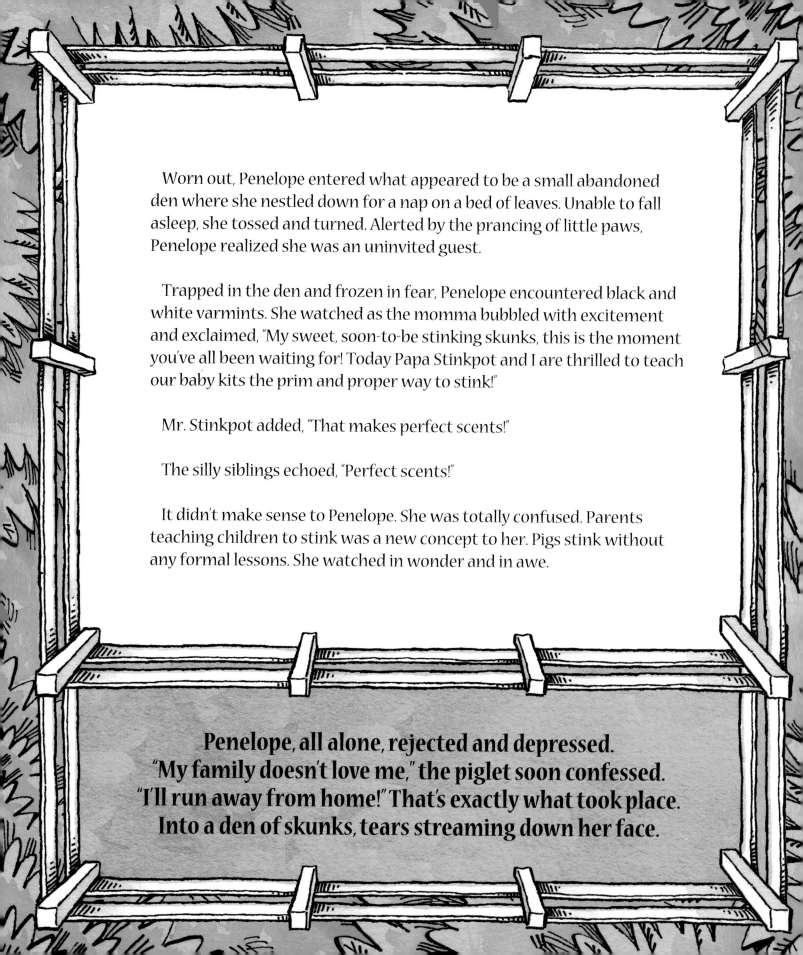

Worn out, Penelope entered what appeared to be a small abandoned den where she nestled down for a nap on a bed of leaves. Unable to fall asleep, she tossed and turned. Alerted by the prancing of little paws, Penelope realized she was an uninvited guest.

Trapped in the den and frozen in fear, Penelope encountered black and white varmints. She watched as the momma bubbled with excitement and exclaimed, "My sweet, soon-to-be stinking skunks, this is the moment you've all been waiting for! Today Papa Stinkpot and I are thrilled to teach our baby kits the prim and proper way to stink!"

Mr. Stinkpot added, "That makes perfect scents!"

The silly siblings echoed, "Perfect scents!"

It didn't make sense to Penelope. She was totally confused. Parents teaching children to stink was a new concept to her. Pigs stink without any formal lessons. She watched in wonder and in awe.

Penelope, all alone, rejected and depressed.
"My family doesn't love me," the piglet soon confessed.
"I'll run away from home!" That's exactly what took place.
Into a den of skunks, tears streaming down her face.

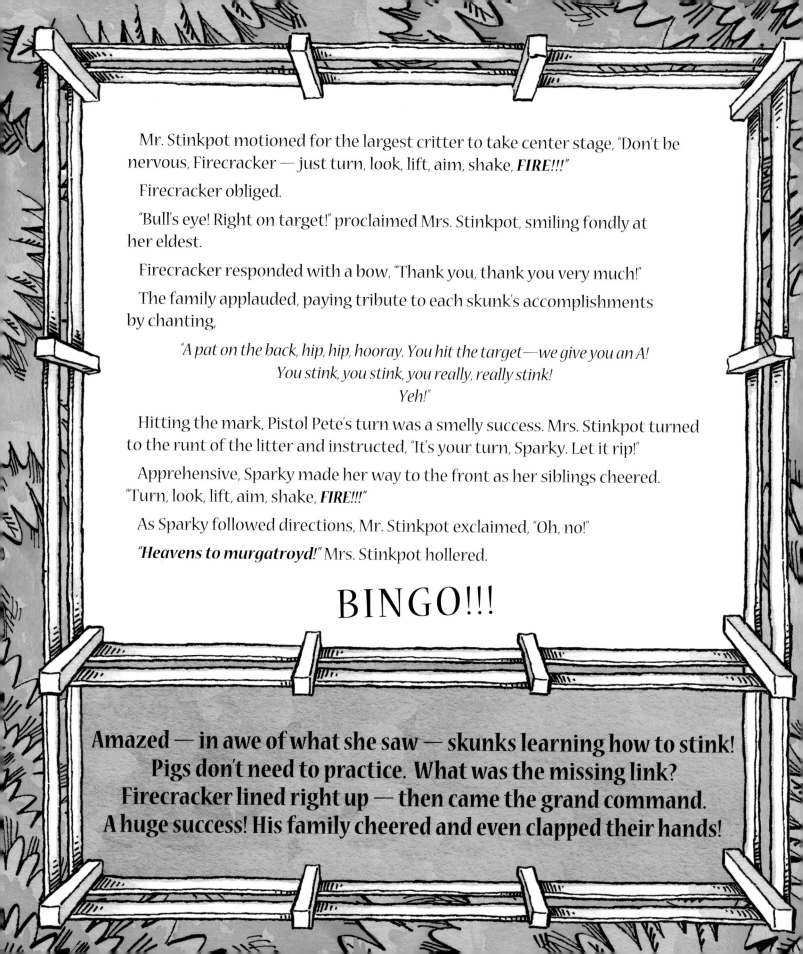

Mr. Stinkpot motioned for the largest critter to take center stage, "Don't be nervous, Firecracker — just turn, look, lift, aim, shake, **FIRE!!!**"

Firecracker obliged.

"Bull's eye! Right on target!" proclaimed Mrs. Stinkpot, smiling fondly at her eldest.

Firecracker responded with a bow, "Thank you, thank you very much!"

The family applauded, paying tribute to each skunk's accomplishments by chanting,

"A pat on the back, hip, hip, hooray. You hit the target—we give you an A!
You stink, you stink, you really, really stink!
Yeh!"

Hitting the mark, Pistol Pete's turn was a smelly success. Mrs. Stinkpot turned to the runt of the litter and instructed, "It's your turn, Sparky. Let it rip!"

Apprehensive, Sparky made her way to the front as her siblings cheered. "Turn, look, lift, aim, shake, **FIRE!!!**"

As Sparky followed directions, Mr. Stinkpot exclaimed, "Oh, no!"

"Heavens to murgatroyd!" Mrs. Stinkpot hollered.

BINGO!!!

Amazed — in awe of what she saw — skunks learning how to stink!
Pigs don't need to practice. What was the missing link?
Firecracker lined right up — then came the grand command.
A huge success! His family cheered and even clapped their hands!

It was the most incredible, unforgettable, remarkable smell ever. Gasping for air, Mr. and Mrs. Stinkpot and all Sparky's siblings cried out,

"P.U. You stink, you stink! You really, really, truly, truly, absolutely, positively stink!"

Stunned, yet manners intact, Sparky replied, "Thank you, thank you very much. I think."

In total shock Sparky watched as her family scurried out of the den. Thoroughly discouraged, she wept, "I'm a skunk! I'm a skunk! I'm supposed to stink! Aren't I?"

Popping up from her bed of leaves, Penelope spoke up, "You do stink. And I should know!"

Startled, Sparky responded, "Who are you?"

"I'm Penelope, a pig, and I stink too!"

Pinching her nose, Sparky concurred. "Tell me about it! What are you doing here?"

Penelope sighed. "I'm running away from home!"

"Running away from home? Won't you miss your family?"

"Yes, but they won't miss me! They can't stand to be around me."

"I know what you mean," Sparky admitted. "Evidently my family can't stand to be around me either. Do you mind if I join you?"

Shaking in her skin and stripes, it was Sparky's turn to try.
The tiny little varmint — the runt — the smallest fry!
Will this stinker have it in her as she took her premiere bow?
Pressure mounting, tensions rising, will her strike be foul?

"Of course you can," declared Penelope. "Hop on board for the best piggyback ride a skunk has ever had! Don't forget to hold onto your stripes!"

Tears poured down their cheeks as, together, they ran away from home. Before long, Penelope realized that running away from home with a skunk on your back was even more exhausting than just running away by herself. She needed to rest her hooves for a while.

Teardrops somewhat obstructing their view, the duo spotted what appeared to be a hollowed-out log and a great place to get some shuteye.

Sparky slipped in with ease. Penelope struggled, swaying back and forth to fit into the tight space. Twisting and turning only made it tighter, which added to Penelope's problems.

One big pig problem!

Her big piggy bottom was just a little too much *behind*. Not only did Penelope stink . . .

Two new friends ran and ran, tears streaming down their face!
Vision blurred, they wandered into Sheriff Stinkbug's place.
Sparky ran right in, her slim body fit just right.
Penelope's big bottom stuck. It was an ugly sight!

. . . She was stuck!

Penelope and Sparky realized that the log wasn't hollow, after all. And to make things worse, the terrified twosome had company. A stone's throw away they heard voices.

"Who turned out the lights? It's pitch dark in here."

"Deputies," Sheriff Stinkbug spoke up, "you have all been given a special, shall we say, 'perfume' to release only—and I repeat **only**—in case of an emergency!"

"Yes, only in case of an emergency," Momma Stinkbug repeated. "We don't want to be too buggy! Hehehehehe!"

The sharp stinkbugs echoed, "Hehehehehe!"

Sheriff Stinkbug cleared his throat and continued, "After bugging the three foxes' hole, the *buzz* is that those evil varmints are planning on eating their main course at Hawg Heaven Farms."

Overhearing this report, Penelope snorted!

Startled by their intruders, the stinkers raised their antennae, positioning their defense mechanisms to strike the trespassers.

"Hold your fire!" Sheriff Stinkbug commanded.

"Hawg Heaven Farm is my home!" sobbed Penelope. "That's my family!"

**Eeeny—Meeny, Miney, Moe, their plot was no surprise.
Sheriff Stinkbug warned his bugs of Hawg Heaven's sure demise.
Penelope spoke right up, "Can't have my family.
Please help me, help me, help me now! It's an emergency!"**

Full of compassion, the sheriff gave Penelope's ear a bug hug and imparted, "Families must stick together. I'm Sheriff Stinkbug. My deputies and I are at your service."

The posse of stinkbugs put their antennae together to devise a scheme. Hearing their ingenious plan, Momma Stinkbug exclaimed, "Perfect! What are we waiting on?"

"Well . . . I'm stuck," Penelope confessed, "which means we're all stuck! There's no way out! We've got **a big pig problem!**"

"**No problem, Penelope!**" Sheriff Stinkbug hollered. "Stinkbugs, this is an emergency. Prepare your weapons!"

The band of bugs raised their antennae, positioned their defense mechanisms and exploded in their infamous stink dance—the *boogie-woogie bug-a-bop bop-hop!* Grooving 'n' a dancing they crooned:

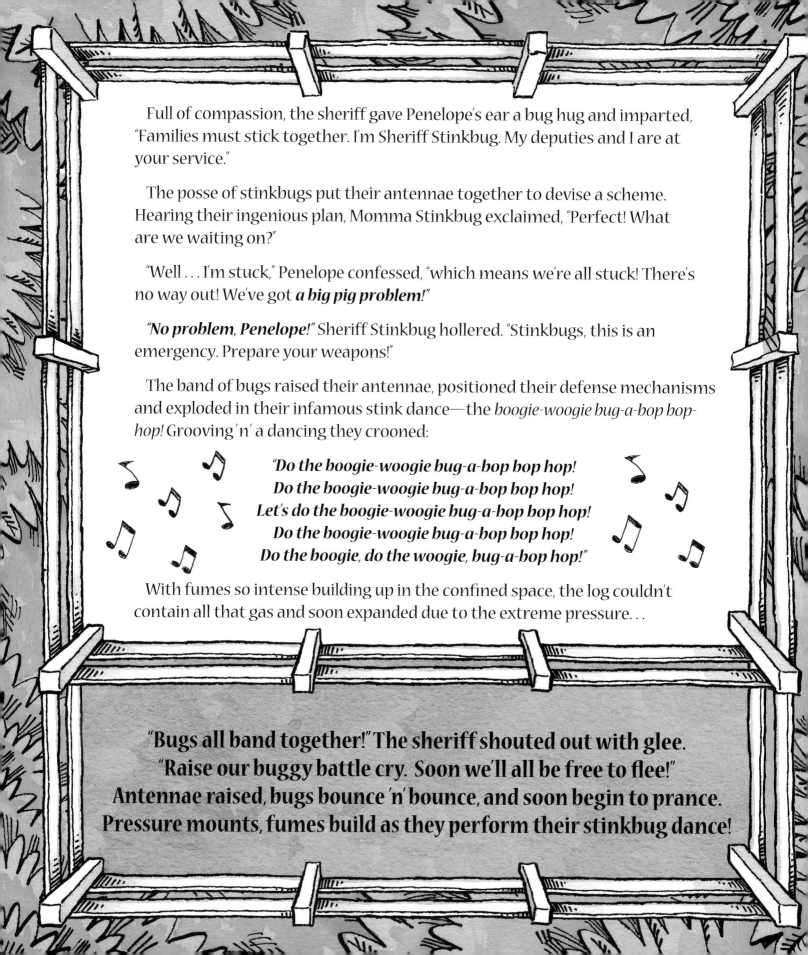

> "***Do the boogie-woogie bug-a-bop bop hop!***
> ***Do the boogie-woogie bug-a-bop bop hop!***
> ***Let's do the boogie-woogie bug-a-bop bop hop!***
> ***Do the boogie-woogie bug-a-bop bop hop!***
> ***Do the boogie, do the woogie, bug-a-bop hop!***"

With fumes so intense building up in the confined space, the log couldn't contain all that gas and soon expanded due to the extreme pressure. . .

"Bugs all band together!" The sheriff shouted out with glee.
"Raise our buggy battle cry. Soon we'll all be free to flee!"
Antennae raised, bugs bounce 'n' bounce, and soon begin to prance.
Pressure mounts, fumes build as they perform their stinkbug dance!

BOOM!!! BOOM!!! BOOM!!!

Back at Hawg Heaven Farms, the three evil foxes, Eeeny–Meeny, Miney and Moe—have the petrified piglets penned in the corner. At their wit's end and trembling in their hooves, Penelope's siblings are on the brink of becoming the foxes' feast.

Drooling, the conniving carnivores chant: …

Boom! Boom!! Boom!!! The log explodes to their delight.
The sheriff mounts his horsefly 'n' shouts with all his might,
"Band together! Raise a stink! Defeat those foxy foes!
Have no fear — to Hawg Heaven Farms — watch those piggy toes!"

Foxes chant in cunning chorus,
"Eeeny, Meeny, Miney, Moe.
Which delicious little porker
will be the first to go?"

Huffin' and a puffin', Penelope arrived just in time, pleading, "Don't eat them—**eat me!**"

Startled by the voice and the awful, putrid, petrifying stench, the foxes chorused, "Why would we want to eat a stinky-poo like you?"

Shrugging her porky shoulders, Penelope stated matter-of-factly, "My family doesn't love me. They can't stand to be around me."

"Oh, you've got it all wrong," her siblings objected. "We do love you! Penelope, you are **the Perfect Pig!**"

"I am?" she questioned. "I thought you said I stink!"

"You do." Pudgy replied. "But that's what pigs are supposed to do. It's just that sometimes we can't stand physically to be around you."

"Rest assured," Pugsy added, "you stink, you stink, you really, really, absolutely, positively stink!"

"But on the other hoof," Potsy butted in, " we really, really, truly, truly, absolutely, positively love you and always will. No ifs, or ands, or buts about it!"

Penelope smiled and sighed. "I get it now!"

"You're going to get it," the fiendish foxes interrupted. **"Ready or not, here we come!"**

Lunging towards Penelope, Eeeny-Meeny, Miney, and Moe slipped. Covered in filth, grime and you-know–what, they sprang to their paws and continued their pursuit of a delicious dinner. Amid total chaos, a faint cry was heard.

Shaking in her skin and stripes, Sparky begged the foxes, "Eat me, eat me!"

Penelope, astounded that her family was in peril,
Ran to shield, protect and guard with one courageous carol!
"We'll work together as a team to defeat this evil foe!
They won't be eating pork today! So on our way we'll go!"

But the evil trio chorused, *"P.U.! You stink!* You really, really stink!"

Manners intact once again, Sparky politely replied. "Thank you. Thank you very much!"

Gasping for breath, Moe asked, "Why would we want to eat you?"

"Because my family doesn't love me. In fact, they left the first time they got *wind* of me."

"I'm not going to let anything happen to you," Penelope declared. *"I love you."*

"And so do we!" chimed in the skunk family.

"But you left me!" complained Sparky.

"We left because *we couldn't breathe,*" Firecracker fired back. "We needed some fresh air."

"You are one remarkable, unforgettable, incredible skunk," Pistol Pete added. "We returned to tell you how very proud of you we were, but you were nowhere in sight."

Mr. Stinkpot popped in, "So we followed your *you-know-what*, and here we are. We do love you. *We really, really, truly, truly, absolutely, positively love you.*"

"Cut it out with all that lovey-dovey stuff!" shouted Eeeny-Meeny.

The foxes pointed their paws and recited, "Eeeny-meeny, miney, moe, what little creature will be the first to go . . ."

"Oh, no you don't!" Sheriff Stinkbug shouted.

"Let the games begin!"

The Stinkpots showed up just in time. "Don't be so alarmed! Our little stinker's smell we've tracked. My dear, you'll not be harmed. This family may be stinkers, but we all must stick together. Sunshine or rain — good or bad — in every kind of weather!"

Those stinkers that had stared in
timid trepidation —
Soon relaxed to watch
Sheriff Stinkbug's
jubilation.

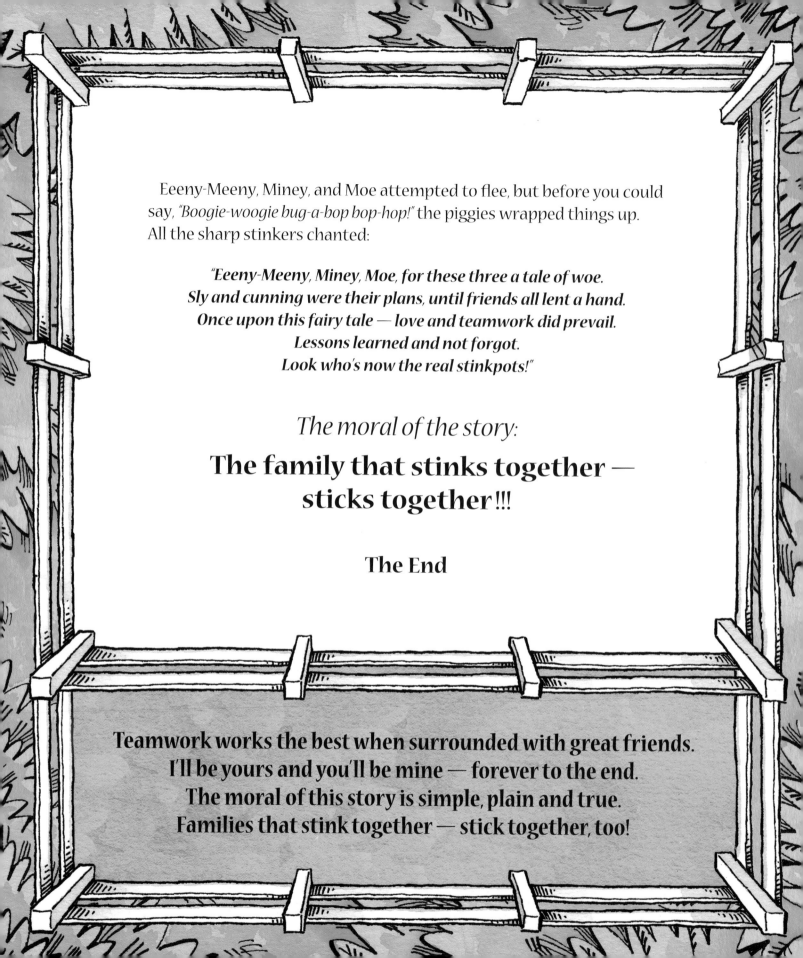

Eeeny-Meeny, Miney, and Moe attempted to flee, but before you could say, *"Boogie-woogie bug-a-bop bop-hop!"* the piggies wrapped things up. All the sharp stinkers chanted:

"Eeeny-Meeny, Miney, Moe, for these three a tale of woe.
Sly and cunning were their plans, until friends all lent a hand.
Once upon this fairy tale — love and teamwork did prevail.
Lessons learned and not forgot.
Look who's now the real stinkpots!"

The moral of the story:

The family that stinks together — sticks together!!!

The End

Teamwork works the best when surrounded with great friends.
I'll be yours and you'll be mine — forever to the end.
The moral of this story is simple, plain and true.
Families that stink together — stick together, too!

As in all Sunflower Seeds Press books—don't forget to find the hidden sunflowers!

ISBN 9780974362762 Hardcover

Text copyright © 2008 'R. Friend' Ronda Friend
Illustrations by Bill Ross — www.billrossdraws.com
Graphic design by Julie Wanca Design — www.juliewancadesign.com

All rights reserved. Published by Sunflower Seeds Press, PO Box 1476, Franklin, Tennessee 37065
Library of Congress Control Number: 2008906932

Printed in the U.S.A.

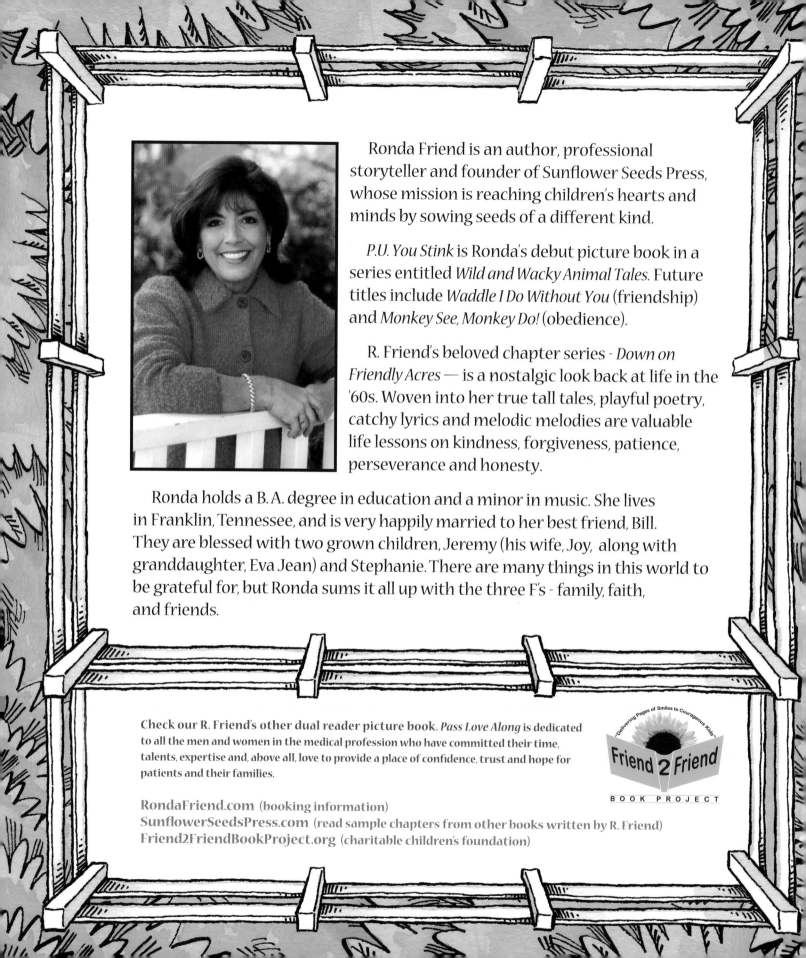

Ronda Friend is an author, professional storyteller and founder of Sunflower Seeds Press, whose mission is reaching children's hearts and minds by sowing seeds of a different kind.

P.U. You Stink is Ronda's debut picture book in a series entitled *Wild and Wacky Animal Tales*. Future titles include *Waddle I Do Without You* (friendship) and *Monkey See, Monkey Do!* (obedience).

R. Friend's beloved chapter series - *Down on Friendly Acres* — is a nostalgic look back at life in the '60s. Woven into her true tall tales, playful poetry, catchy lyrics and melodic melodies are valuable life lessons on kindness, forgiveness, patience, perseverance and honesty.

Ronda holds a B.A. degree in education and a minor in music. She lives in Franklin, Tennessee, and is very happily married to her best friend, Bill. They are blessed with two grown children, Jeremy (his wife, Joy, along with granddaughter, Eva Jean) and Stephanie. There are many things in this world to be grateful for, but Ronda sums it all up with the three F's - family, faith, and friends.

Check our R. Friend's other dual reader picture book. *Pass Love Along* is dedicated to all the men and women in the medical profession who have committed their time, talents, expertise and, above all, love to provide a place of confidence, trust and hope for patients and their families.

RondaFriend.com (booking information)
SunflowerSeedsPress.com (read sample chapters from other books written by R. Friend)
Friend2FriendBookProject.org (charitable children's foundation)

"Delivering Pages of Smiles to Courageous Kids"

Friend 2 Friend
B O O K   P R O J E C T